Pilot Bird and Gu

Story by Jon Blake

Pictures by Rowan Barnes Murphy

Deep down in the deep, dark, dense jungle, there was a wide river. It was a river of crocodiles.

They lay in the sun, they swam in the river and they yawned with their huge, toothy, crocodile mouths.

No one would ever dare get close to a crocodile's mouth. No one, that is, except Pilot Bird. Pilot Bird got just as close as she wanted. In fact, Pilot Bird hopped right inside and pecked scraps from the crocodiles' teeth.

The crocodiles never tried to eat Pilot Bird. Pilot Bird was their toothbrush. Thanks to Pilot Bird, the crocodiles all had gleaming white teeth and fresh breath. Thanks to the crocodiles, Pilot Bird had lunch whenever she wanted.

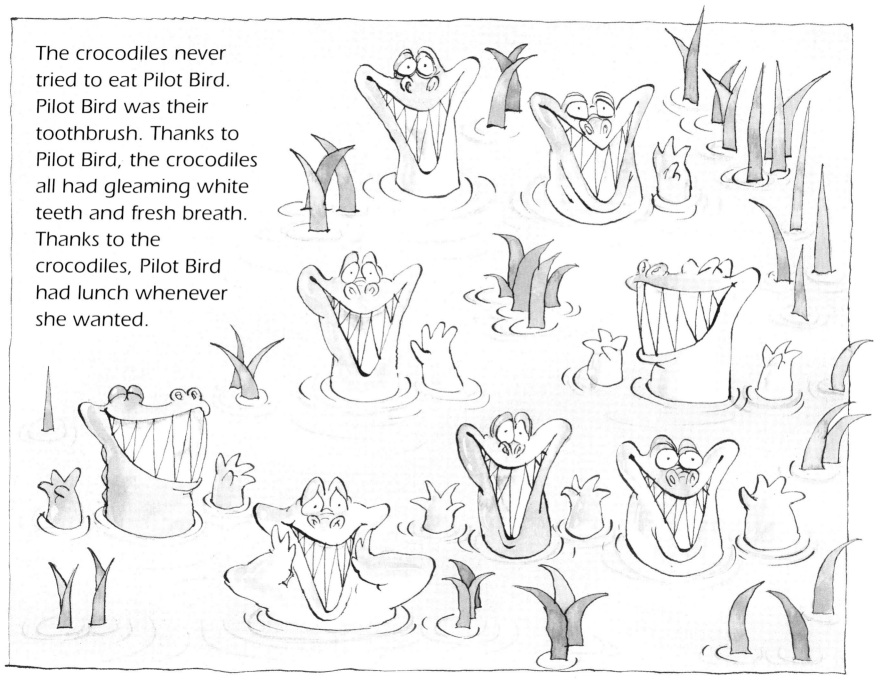

One day, a new crocodile came to the river. He wasn't quite like the other crocodiles. He kept himself to himself and took no notice of the Pilot Bird.

'Open up!' said the Pilot Bird, hopping onto his nose.

But the new crocodile would not open up.

'I'll clean my own teeth, thank you,' he muttered.

The new crocodile sat on the riverbank and picked his teeth with a stick. But there were so many teeth, he soon got fed up.

'Who needs clean teeth anyway?' he said to himself.

Every night and every
morning, Pilot Bird
hopped onto the new
crocodile's nose.

'Open up!' she said,
each time.

But the new crocodile
would not open up.

'My teeth are just fine,
thank you,' he muttered.

One night, there was a howl which was heard all through the jungle. The new crocodile had got toothache.

'Now will you let me clean your teeth?' said Pilot Bird.

'I'll be better tomorrow, thank you,' groaned the new crocodile.

But the new crocodile was not better tomorrow.
In fact, he got worse, and worse, and worse.
Soon all this teeth ached.

One tooth fell out.

Then another.

Then another.

In the end, he had no teeth left at all.

'Serves you right!' said the other crocodiles.

They decided to call him Gums.

Gums felt very sorry for himself. He sat all day in the gloomy shade, pining for his lost teeth. He couldn't eat anything but soup. And there wasn't a lot of soup in the jungle.

'What can I do?' he moaned.

Pilot Bird took pity on Gums, even though he didn't deserve it.

'Come with me,' she said. 'We'll find the jungle dentist, and get you some false teeth.'

Pilot Bird and Gums set off in search of the jungle dentist.

They passed Magic Monkey, showing off his magic tricks.

They crossed the great grasslands, past giraffes and antelopes and zebras.

They walked along the edge of the great lake, where the pink flamingoes were.

At last they reached a wooden hut, with a sign
outside which said MR SNAPPER - JUNGLE DENTIST.

Gums looked in through
the window.

'Help! It's a crocodile!'
yelled one of the animals.

All the animals jumped,
and screamed, and stampeded
out of the back door.

'I'm not going to <u>that</u>
dentist,' said Gums.
'All his patients look scared stiff.'

Nothing could persuade Gums to go into the dentist's hut.

Pilot Bird and Gums began the long walk back, feeling tired and hungry. But Pilot Bird couldn't eat unless Gums ate, and Gums couldn't eat because he had no false teeth.

Then they came across Magic Monkey again. He was sitting in the gloomy shade with his head in his hands. He looked even more miserable than Gums and Pilot Bird.

'What's the matter, Magic Monkey?' asked Pilot Bird.

'It's my magic necklace,' said Magic Monkey. 'It doesn't work any more.'

Magic Monkey pulled a
long, spiky necklace
from his pocket.
   Gums couldn't believe it.
   The necklace was
made of crocodile teeth.

Pilot Bird stroked her chin and thought for a while. Then she had an idea.

'If you give me that necklace,' she said, 'I'll give you one of my feathers.'

'Why should I want one of your feathers?' asked Magic Monkey.

'My feathers are magic,' said Pilot Bird. 'With these feathers, I can hop right into a crocodile's mouth.'

'Oh no you can't' scoffed Magic Monkey.

'Oh yes I can,' said Pilot Bird.

Pilot Bird jumped onto Gums's nose.

'Open up!' she said.

This time, Gums opened his mouth wide. Pilot Bird hopped inside.

Magic Monkey was so amazed, he didn't even
notice Gums had no teeth.
  'Here!' said Magic Monkey. 'Have the necklace!
Just give me one of your feathers!'

Pilot Bird plucked a feather from her tail, and swapped it for the tooth-necklace.

Magic Monkey stuck the feather in his hat, and went leaping and jumping and swinging through the forest, shouting 'I'm magic! I'm magic everybody!'

Now Gums has a new set of teeth, as white and sharp as any in the jungle. And this time, he's going to keep them that way.

With the help of his toothbrush, of course.

FORESTRY COMMISSION BULLETIN 91

The Timbers of Farm Woodland Trees

J. D. Brazier

formerly of the Princes Risborough Laboratory,
Building Research Establishment,
Department of the Environment

LONDON: HMSO

ISBN 0 11 710284 9
ODC 83: 264: (410)

KEYWORDS: Wood utilisation, Woodlands, Forestry

Enquiries relating to this publication
should be addressed to:
The Technical Publications Officer,
Forestry Commission, Forest Research Station,
Alice Holt Lodge, Wrecclesham,
Farnham, Surrey GU10 4LH.

Front Cover: Mature sycamore being harvested
at Dalby Hall Farm, Lincolnshire. *(39282)*

Contents

The Timbers of Farm Woodland Trees

Summary

Farmers are being encouraged to grow trees on surplus agricultural land as part of government policy effected through the Farm Woodland Scheme. The efficient production of timber is profitable, providing raw material for industry, yet it does not preclude other important objectives such as landscape design, amenity considerations, game management and wildlife conservation. The production of high quality timber is paramount if investment in woodlands is to be realised. This Bulletin describes the characteristics and uses of 15 hardwood and 8 softwood timbers of trees suitable for farm woodland planting.

Le Bois des Forêts de Ferme

Résumé

On encourage les agriculteurs à cultiver des arbres sur les zones agricoles en surplus, ce qui fait partie de la politique du gouvernement effective grâce au Projet Forêts de Ferme. La production efficace du bois fournissant des matières premières à l'industrie est rentable, mais elle n'exclut pas d'autres buts importants tel que l'esthétique du paysage, les possibilités de récréation, la préservation du gibier et la conservation de la nature. La production du bois de haute qualité est d'une importance extrême, si on veut investir dans les forêts. Ce Bulletin décrit les caractéristiques et les usages du bois de 15 feuillus et 8 résineux convenables à la culture dans les forêts de ferme.

Die Hölzer von Bauernwaldbäumen

Zusammenfassung

Landwirte werden jetzt durch ein Programm der Regierungspolitik: dem Bauern-
waldanschlag angetrieben, Bäume auf überschüssigem landwirtschaftlich
genutztem Land zu kultivieren. Leistungsfähige Holzproduktion, die Rohstoffe
für die Industrie erzeugt, ist nützlich, jedoch andere wichtige Ziele wie
Landschaftsplanung, Erholungszwecke, Wildwirtschaft und Naturschutz sind
dabei nicht ausgeschlossen. Die Produktion von Qualitätsholz ist ausschlagge-
bend, wenn Investitionen für Waldflächen benötigt werden. Dieses Bulletin
beschreibt die Merkmale und Verwendungen von Baumarten (15 Laubhölzer und
8 Nadelhölzer), die für Bauernwaldanbau geeignet sind.

Foreword

This Bulletin has been prepared as a compact source of information on timber utilisation for those managing or establishing farm woodlands. Its author Dr J. D. Brazier, until recently a member of the Princes Risborough Laboratory of the Building Research Establishment, has immense experience of timber properties and uses.

A word of caution is necessary in relation to preparation of trees or roundwood for specific products. Timber conversion is, except for the simplest products such as firewood or fence stakes, not a simple matter. It is essential that a grower should become familiar with the market he intends to supply and its specifications and it is recommended that competent advice be taken before entering on any utilisation.

I am grateful to Mr J. C. Peters, Rural Affairs Directorate, Department of the Environment, for suggesting the preparation of this short compendium and to Dr J. W. W. Morgan of the Building Research Establishment who arranged its completion by Dr Brazier.

A. J. Grayson
Former Director of Research,
Forestry Commission

Plate 1.
Gates and fencing
stakes produced from
home-grown timber.
(*E8432*)

Plate 2.
Square timber and
fencing on a farm.
(*39307*)

Plate 3.
Pallets constructed from
home-grown timber. (*E7994*)

Plate 4.
Lettuce crate made from
home-grown softwood
and poplar. (*3576*)

Plate 5.
Softwood
transmission poles
treated with CCA
preservative. (*37656*)

Plate 6.
Battens of home-grown timber being fed into a machine stress grader for testing. (*E8682*)

Plate 7.
Small roundwood for pulping – hardwood logs at the rideside. (*E7128*)

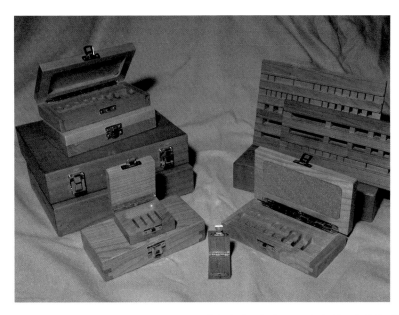

Plate 8.
A selection of instrument cases and inserts manufactured from cherry timber. These precision-made cases are for export to Switzerland. (*39302*)

Plate 9.
Hampshire-grown cherry timber and a small stack of walnut from trees windblown in the storm of October 1987. The timber is stacked for drying; the first lengths were ready for use in April 1990. (*39300*)

Plate 10.
The Ercol Windsor Chairmaker's Chair. The seat is made from elm, the bentwood pieces, sticks and legs are of beech. (© *Ercol Furniture Ltd.*)

The Timbers of Farm Woodland Trees

J. D. Brazier, formerly of the Princes Risborough Laboratory, Building Research Establishment, Department of the Environment

Introduction

This Bulletin describes the properties and uses of timbers of trees suitable for farm woodland planting.

A farmer growing trees can reasonably expect to sell or use the timber, but growing for sale to the timber market requires care in selection and attention to growth. In the first place, trees that suit the site must be chosen and advice and guidance should be sought from professional foresters or from the literature (Forestry Commission Bulletin 80 *Farm woodland planning*, Forestry Commission Handbook 3 *Farm woodland practice*, set of ADAS/FC leaflets *Practical work in farm woods*). Choice should favour timbers that are commonly used and are acceptable for a variety of purposes, as it is easier to market and, often, to obtain a higher price for timbers with established markets than for those with an occasional demand or which are commonly sold in mixture with similar woods. The timber trees can be *grown* in mixture with other species, planted for amenity, ground cover and so on, but silvicultural management should favour the commercial species where timber production is the objective.

Straight, cylindrical stems must be grown if marketability is not to be severely limited. Selecting the best trees when thinning for the final crop and removing dead and suppressed branches from the lower stem while the trees are small can improve quality. Quality is particularly important with hardwoods used for purposes where appearance, stability or strength matter, as in furniture and joinery. Misshapen or damaged trees, if saleable, fetch a low price as they are suitable only for rough work, fuelwood, or, if within acceptable limits of size, for pulpwood.

Softwoods grow more quickly than most hardwoods and reach a larger size sooner. They generally command lower prices per unit volume than well grown hardwoods but yields per hectare are higher. British grown sawn softwood is used mainly for building, fencing and estate work, and for pallets and packaging. Most softwoods are suitable for these purposes and, if well grown, meet the quality requirements and are readily accepted. Small roundwood stems are particularly useful for farm and estate purposes though their main commercial uses are in pulp, board products and for pitwood. Users issue specifications giving acceptable timbers, sizes and other requirements for these purposes.

Brief notes are given for each timber. For more detailed information on properties and uses of British timbers, reference should be made to:

Handbook of hardwoods, 2nd Edition (1972), HMSO, London, price £20.00;
A handbook of softwoods, 2nd Edition (1977), HMSO, London, price £8.00.

Hardwoods

Hardwoods are the timbers of broadleaved trees which, in a temperate country such as Britain, are normally deciduous, losing their leaves in the winter months. Despite their name, hardwoods vary in weight and hardness. Some, such as oak and beech, are hard and heavy, slow growing and long lived; others, such as poplar and willow, grow quickly and have lightweight, 'soft' woods.

Alder (*Alnus* species)

Alder produces a uniformly pale, somewhat featureless wood which darkens to pale orange-brown on exposure and has a fine texture and

1

generally straight grain. It is of medium weight, with strength properties approaching those of Scots pine.

Alder dries rapidly and well. It saws easily and machines to a good finish with sharp cutters. It is soon attacked by fungi in conditions favouring decay but is easily treated with preservative solutions.

The timber is never available in quantity or large sizes and it is used for general purpose items such as brush and broom backs, toys, turnery, often in mixture with similar light-weight, pale woods. Traditionally alder is used for clogs and it has been used for artificial limbs. Alder needs preservative treatment for most estate uses, is accepted for hardwood pulp, but is not a good fuelwood although it can make a high quality charcoal.

Ash (*Fraxinus excelsior*)

Ash typically produces a white wood though, on wet or other unfavourable growth sites, it can develop a core of dark wood, which is disliked by users. Growth rings are conspicuous giving clean white wood a particularly attractive figure. The wood is heavy, comparable to beech, although the weight varies depending on vigour of growth.

It is an easy wood to handle as it dries readily and can be sawn and machined to a good finish; once dry it is fairly stable in use. Ash is stronger than oak but, unlike oak, not durable in conditions favouring decay unless treated with preservative.

Ash is the toughest of British grown woods and many of its uses (such as for pick, axe and hammer handles, shafts of spades, forks, rakes and similar tools, rungs of ladders, tent pegs, sports goods, cricket stumps, etc.) require toughness. British ash from straight, vigorous growth trees is preferred to ash from elsewhere. Good quality ash is used in furniture and outstanding trees for veneer. It is a useful estate timber, though not for use in ground contact unless treated; it is accepted for pulp and makes an excellent fuelwood.

Beech (*Fagus sylvatica*)

Beech is white when first cut but becomes a very pale brown on drying and exposure. Well grown,

it is straight-grained, with a fine texture and a characteristic ray figure which, if much less obvious than that in oak, is seen on both flat sawn and radial surfaces. Beech is a heavy wood, comparable in weight to a tough oak, and is one of the strongest British timbers.

Beech kiln dries quickly and well although with a large shrinkage and, once dry, it tends to move more than most British timbers under changing conditions of humidity. It is not durable where there is a decay risk but is readily treated with preservatives.

Available at modest cost and in good supply, both from Britain and elsewhere in Europe, beech is the most commonly used hardwood in Britain. It is the foremost furniture wood, especially for chairs and tables, as it machines well, is strong and has a uniform pale appearance suitable for a variety of finishes. Wood of good quality – straight grained, clean and free from growth defects – is sought for most furniture, but somewhat lower quality is used for the framing of upholstered furniture. Beech is used for tool handles and other turned items, domestic ware, especially kitchen-ware, for toys, and it makes a hard wearing domestic floor. Timber from mis-shapen trees can be difficult to market but it makes excellent firewood and in appropriate sizes is accepted for hardwood pulp.

Birch (*Betula pendula, B. pubescens*)

The two species have similar, almost white, somewhat featureless, fine textured woods. Well grown trees have a straight grain but those colonising open ground are often of poor form with an irregular grain. The wood is moderately heavy but not quite the weight of beech.

Birch dries readily but with a large shrinkage and a tendency to distort. It saws and machines to give a good finish, although the finish is better when the grain is straight. It is a strong wood, almost as tough as ash when dry. The wood is perishable in conditions favouring decay but is readily treated with preservatives.

Because of its frequent poor form, British grown birch is generally inferior to that from Scandinavia, which is most familiar as plywood. In the round, British timber is used mainly for pulp or as fuelwood. Sawnwood is used for turned items, such as bobbins and spools, brush and broom backs, pegs, wooden toys and the like, for pallets and in furniture, good quality for exposed parts, lower grades for the framing of upholstered items. The fine branches of birch are used for besoms, for steeplechase jumps, thatching and weaving.

Cherry (*Prunus avium*)

Cherry has a pinkish-brown heartwood with a well defined paler sapwood, typically straight grained and with a fine, even texture. Cherry is somewhat lighter in weight than beech and not quite as strong.

Cherry needs to be dried carefully as it tends to distort but, once dry, is fairly stable in use. Cherry works well taking an excellent finish. It is moderately durable in conditions favouring decay but, generally, should not be considered for outdoor use.

It is a most attractive wood available in limited supply and only modest sizes. Cherry is sought by craftsmen for cabinet making and furniture, for panelling and decorative joinery. It has an assured market and is unlikely to be in over-supply but must be well grown as timber marred by growth blemishes is difficult to market for other than low grade uses.

Hornbeam (*Carpinus betulus*)

Hornbeam has a uniformly white wood with a very fine texture and, often, somewhat irregular grain. One of the most dense British hardwoods, heavier than beech but, in many ways, like a dense, pale beech. It dries fairly quickly but with a large shrinkage, has a tendency to distort and is not particularly stable once dry. It is a strong, tough wood which wears very evenly and smoothly. Although it is somewhat harder to saw and machine than beech, it finishes to an excellent surface. It is perishable in conditions favouring decay but can be readily treated with preservatives.

For the most part available in small sizes, often from coppice, and in only modest quantities, hornbeam is used mainly for pulpwood or fuelwood, including charcoal. It is of little use as an estate timber except where a hard-wearing surface is needed. Straight grained timber

makes good tool handles and traditional uses include wearing parts in wind- and water-mills and for piano actions. Selected timber should make an attractive, hard-wearing floor.

Lime (*Tilia* species)

Lime produces an almost white wood which darkens to a honey colour on exposure; it has a very fine and even texture and hardly any growth ring figure. Lime is one of the lighter weight British hardwoods but with good strength for its weight.

Lime dries quickly and well though with a tendency to distort but, once dry, it is fairly stable in use. It works well with all tools and can be machined to an excellent finish. It is perishable in conditions favouring decay but can be readily treated with preservatives.

Lime is an attractive pale wood which could find wider use for purposes requiring modest strength and plain appearance if it were more readily available. Traditionally, lime is used for hat blocks, beehive frames and piano parts and with other pale woods for brushes, turned items such as toys and bobbins, and dairy and domestic items. It is an exceptional wood for carving, often preferred to others for its ease of working and the fine detail which can be obtained. Small roundwood is accepted for hardwood pulp.

Norway maple (*Acer platanoides*)

Norway maple is closely related to and like sycamore in colour, grain and texture, but marginally harder and heavier. It saws, dries and machines like sycamore and is not durable for outdoor use unless given a preservative treatment.

Norway maple is used for the same purposes as sycamore but, because it is usually available in somewhat smaller sizes, it tends to go into turned items, kitchen-ware, etc. or for pulpwood or fuelwood.

Nothofagus
Rauli (*Nothofagus procera*)
Roble (*Nothofagus obliqua*)

Nothofagus produces mostly pale sapwood with small amounts of coloured heartwood, cherrywood-like in rauli but more drab in roble.

The wood is fine textured and generally straight-grained; it has a marked tendency to split along the grain on felling and in later processing. Rauli is fairly light in weight, comparable to alder; roble is heavier, nearer the weight of sycamore.

Although it is somewhat slow to dry, once dry rauli has very good stability in service. Both timbers saw easily and clear timber machines to a good finish. The large amount of sapwood is perishable in conditions favouring decay but should accept preservative treatments.

These timbers are sometimes known as southern hemisphere beech, but they are appreciably weaker than beech and differ from it in appearance. As sawn wood, they are suitable for purposes for which other light to medium weight hardwoods are used but have no particular merits to find a special purpose market. For estate use, the large amount of sapwood requires preservative treatment. Roundwood is accepted for hardwood pulp.

Oak (*Quercus robur, Q. petraea*)

The best-known British wood, oak is pale brown, coarse-textured, typically straight grained and with a conspicuous silver-grain figure when quarter sawn; it has a well-defined, pale sapwood. Oak is more variable in character than most woods, with British timber typically heavy, strong and tough from vigorous growth trees; that from old or slowly grown trees is softer and milder. The two species have similar woods which are not distinguished commercially.

Oak dries slowly, with care needed in kiln drying to avoid degrade. Sawing and ease of working depend on density. Heartwood has excellent decay resistance but sapwood is perishable, is liable to insect attack and must be excluded or given preservative treatment if long-term service is required.

Oak varies greatly in quality, depending on straightness of grain and presence of knots, epicormics, internal splits, stain, etc., with the best timber commanding a price ten times that of the poorest. Top quality logs are used for veneer and other high quality timber in furniture, joinery, panelling, flooring and ships' planking. Large sections are used in heavy construction, boat building, canal and harbour works. Lesser quality oak is sawn for estate, farm and garden uses, for posts, fencing and where there is a need for decay resistance. Galvanised fastenings should be used as the heartwood corrodes iron in moist conditions. Roundwood is split for posts, is accepted for hardwood pulp and makes excellent firewood.

Poplar
Black hybrids (*Populus* × *euramericana*)
Balsam poplars (cultivars of *Populus trichocarpa* and *P. balsamifera*)

Poplars are characterised by a variety of cultivars and advice should be sought on selection for planting.

Most poplar cultivars have a similar wood, soft, white, very fine textured and straight grained. Differences are associated with form and vigour of the tree, with the best wood coming from straight, cylindrical stems; poor form results in cross-grain, a woolly finish and a marked tendency for the wood to distort. Poplar is one of the lightest weight British hardwoods with strength properties comparable to those of a softwood such as spruce.

Poplar dries fairly rapidly and well. It saws easily but cutters must be kept sharp to give a good finish when machined; it is peeled for veneer. It is perishable in conditions favouring decay and the heartwood is resistant to preservative treatment by pressure methods.

Sawn poplar is a useful general purpose wood for indoor use where strength is not of major concern. It tends to crush rather than splinter under load and has good abrasion resistance for domestic flooring and truck and waggon bottoms. It is used for pallets and containers, particularly for one-trip items. Poplar is peeled for veneer for chip baskets and vegetable crates. Small roundwood is accepted for hardwood pulp and poplar is the main timber for wafer board and oriented strand board in North America, though not, as yet, used for such boards in Britain.

Sweet chestnut (*Castanea sativa*)

Sweet chestnut produces an attractive, warm yellow-brown wood resembling a plain oak in colour and texture but lacking the silver grain figure of oak; there is a very narrow, pale sapwood ring, much less than in oak. The grain is straight in young stems but tends to spiral as the tree ages. Sweet chestnut is of medium weight, some 20 per cent lighter than oak and correspondingly lower in strength.

It dries slowly and care is needed to avoid degrade; once dry, it is one of the most stable British woods. It is easier to saw and machine than oak and, like oak, the heartwood has an excellent resistance to decay.

Sweet chestnut is an attractive, underrated wood obtained from coppice and larger trees, though old trees tend to have internal splits and spiral grain. With a minimal sapwood, coppice stems make excellent stakes and poles for estate work, though galvanised fastenings should be used as the heartwood corrodes iron in moist conditions. Sawnwood makes durable posts, gates, etc. and the wood is cleft for fencing. Select wood is used for exterior and interior joinery and for furniture; fine logs command a good price for veneer.

Sycamore (*Acer pseudoplatanus*)

Sycamore has an almost white wood with a distinctive growth ring figure on flat sawn surfaces and a high natural lustre, especially on quarter sawn stock. The texture is fine and even and the grain generally straight, but occasionally wavy giving a characteristic fiddle-back figure. Somewhat lighter in weight than beech and not as strong.

Sycamore dries rapidly and well but care is needed in kiln drying to retain a white colour and protracted air drying can result in staining; once dry, it is fairly stable in use and works well to give an excellent finish. Sycamore is quickly damaged by fungi in conditions favouring decay but it is easily treated with preservatives.

Sycamore is an attractive, blond wood used in cabinet work and for furniture framing. The wood is also popular for kitchen items, bread and chopping boards, for dairy items, and for wooden rollers, brush handles and the like. Small round-wood is used for pulp and burns well when dry, though it is not as dense as some other hardwoods. Outstanding logs and especially those with a wavy grain are cut for veneer and command a high price.

Walnut
European walnut (*Juglans regia*)
American walnut (*Juglans nigra*)

Walnut is one of the world's outstanding decorative woods. European walnut can have a highly figured heartwood, greyish-brown with irregular, almost black streaks. American walnut, though highly valued, it is not so figured, typically a more uniform purplish-brown, darkening with age. Only the heartwood is figured; the sapwood is plain but often used. The wood has a medium texture and straight or occasionally wavy grain which enhances the figure. Walnut is somewhat lighter in weight than beech and not quite as strong.

The wood dries slowly but well and it saws easily and machines to an excellent finish. The heartwood is resistant to decay but the sapwood is liable to insect attack.

Walnut is a tree where quality is particularly important. Always in limited supply, logs with figured wood command high prices for veneer, which is used mainly in cabinet work and decorative panelling. Solid wood is used for high class joinery, for the butts and stocks of rifles and sporting guns, and for turned items and craft work.

Willow (*Salix* species)

The different species of willow have similar woods, mostly white, featureless and with a very fine texture, similar to that of the poplars. Comparable to poplar in weight but marginally weaker in most strength properties; cricket bat willow is particular light in weight but absorbs energy without splintering.

Willow dries quickly and well and, once dry, is particularly stable in use. It saws easily and finishes well given sharp cutters; it is perishable in conditions favouring decay and the heartwood resists pressure treatments with preservatives.

The only important timber tree is cricket bat willow, a special cultivar of white willow, which if grown rapidly to give a clean, straight-grained wood, is sought for bat blades. Other solid wood uses include artificial limbs, floors and waggon bottoms, as willow tends to crush rather than splinter. Selected willows are grown for the young shoots. On wet soils, osiers are cut each year to give slender stems for wickerwork and basketwork, and at river sides, trees pollarded every few years at about head height give thicker shoots for stakes and hurdles.

Softwoods

Softwoods are the timbers of coniferous or cone bearing trees with needle-shaped or scale-like leaves which, in most trees, persist for several years so the trees are evergreen. Only the larches, among the softwoods described below, lose all their leaves each winter.

Most softwoods are light- to medium-weight and are not as strong as the heavier hardwoods. Typically they are also more knotty and so tend to be used for more utility purposes.

Douglas fir (*Pseudotsuga menziesii*)

Douglas fir is like pine in appearance but with a pinkish colour, narrower sapwood and more conspicuous growth ring figure; it can be knotty with, often, large knots as branches tend to be long lived. It is marginally heavier than pine, is comparable in stiffness but not quite as strong.

The wood dries quickly and well. It saws and machines easily, though the quality of finish is affected by the size and number of knots; it tends to split on nailing. Heartwood is moderately durable, comparable to that of pine; it is more difficult to treat with preservatives than pine but, when treated, gives excellent service out of doors.

Douglas fir is a most useful wood. On favourable sites, the tree grows quickly to a large size giving a strong timber available in large sections and long lengths. Such baulks are used for piling, for pier, dock and harbour work, and for building where a wide span is sought, as in barns and similar storage sheds. Sawn to smaller sections, it is used for general building purposes, fencing posts, rails, gates and other farm and estate work. Roundwood is useful for farm and estate use but should be treated; it is not favoured for pulp and chipboard use.

Fir
Grand fir (*Abies grandis*)
Noble fir (*Abies procera*)

The firs are white woods, very like spruce in appearance, but with a slight greyish tint and not as lustrous. Usually fast grown, the wood has a coarse texture and generally larger knots than those in spruce. It is marginally lighter in weight than spruce and is one of the weakest of British timbers.

The firs dry quickly and well and when dry are stable in use. The wood saws easily but sharp cutters are needed for a good finish; it nails well. The timber is not resistant to fungi in conditions favouring decay and is difficult to treat effectively with preservatives.

With only a limited supply, there is no established market for British-grown fir. It can be used for the same purposes as spruce, though it is somewhat weaker and is not as acceptable as a construction timber. It is used for pulp and board products.

Larch
European larch (*Larix decidua*)
Hybrid larch (*Larix* × *eurolepis*)
Japanese larch (*Larix kaempferi*)

The larches have similar woods, though slow growth timber from old European larch is heavier and often darker than the younger and typically more rapid growth wood of much Japanese and hybrid larch, commonly planted today. Larch is marginally heavier than pine, with heartwood of a similar, yellow to red-brown colour, but with a much narrower band of pale sapwood. Many, fairly small dead knots are a common feature of the wood due to branches which die early and persist, though these branches are easily removed by brashing or pruning.

Larch is somewhat slower drying than pine but when dry is more stable. It is harder to saw and machine than pine and tends to split on nailing. It lasts outdoors better than pine but, where a long life is sought, a preservative treatment should be given.

Larch is primarily an estate timber, used for buildings, gates, posts and fencing, including close-boarded fencing, and a continuing demand for these purposes is likely. Select larch is a preferred timber for boat building and quality logs can expect an assured market. It is a good, general purpose building timber, comparable in strength to pine. Small roundwood is best used for farm and estate work as it is not liked for pulp or board uses.

Lawson cypress (*Chamaecyparis lawsoniana*)

The wood is a pale yellow-brown with a fine, even texture and a pleasant scent. It is comparable in weight to spruce, with similar strength properties but is lower in stiffness.

It is reported to dry well and to be stable in use. It saws easily and machines to a good finish; it takes nails well. Heartwood has a good resistance to fungi in conditions favouring decay.

The supply of British-grown timber has been so small that there is no established market. Like western red cedar, Lawson cypress combines natural durability and good stability and is best used where these properties are sought, for greenhouse and shed frames, stagings, boxes for outdoor use (though not foodstuffs), cladding and facings. Small roundwood makes a serviceable post or pole but the permeable sapwood should have a preservative treatment.

Pine
Scots pine (*Pinus sylvestris*)
Corsican pine (*Pinus nigra* var. *maritima*)
Lodgepole pine (*Pinus contorta*)

Scots and Corsican pines, though readily distinguished as trees and in log form, have similar woods which are described together; lodgepole pine is somewhat different and is considered separately.

Scots and Corsican pines are medium-weight, mildly resinous softwoods, typically with a conspicuous growth-ring figure and somewhat coarse texture. Most timber is somewhat knotty, with generally larger and more distinctively whorled knots in Corsican pine. Heartwood is yellow- to red-brown and clearly distinguished from the pale sapwood which is often wide, particularly in Corsican pine.

The pines dry quickly and well and once dry are stable in use. They saw and work well, taking a good finish, and can be nailed without splitting. The wood is not resistant to decay but is readily treated with preservatives; the sapwood is liable to stain if log extraction, conversion and drying are delayed in spring and summer months.

It is a most useful and versatile wood. Sawnwood is used in building construction, for packaging and pallets, and for estate work. Roundwood is used for telegraph and transmission poles, after appropriate treatment, and, in smaller sizes, for fencing posts and stakes. It is an important pulp wood and is used in particleboards, including oriented strand board.

Lodgepole pine is a milder, more even textured wood, not quite as strong as the other pines and with a somewhat paler heartwood. Wood quality is particularly affected by stem form, as some trees have a marked tendency to basal sweep.

The wood processes well. It dries quickly and machines easily, taking an exceptionally good finish. It is not durable and, like other pines, the sapwood is particularly susceptible to stain if conversion and drying are delayed.

It is little used in Britain, as yet, but is potentially useful for most purposes for which Scots and Corsican pine are used. With a more even texture, straight grained timber with few and small knots could find favour for joinery and furniture.

Spruce
Norway spruce (*Picea abies*)
Sitka spruce (*Picea sitchensis*)

The spruces have similar, uniformly white woods, sometimes slightly pink in Sitka, which also tends to somewhat faster growth; they are among the lighter-weight softwoods. The timber is not as resinous as pine and, though generally knotty, the knots are smaller than those in pine.

Spruce dries quickly and well. It saws readily and machines easily, though the finish is not always as good as with pine; it nails well. Spruce is not resistant to decay and, when dry, is difficult to treat with preservative solutions; wet wood can be treated by allowing preservative salts to diffuse into the wood.

Spruce is the most abundant timber from

British forests. It is sawn for pallet boards and packaging and in increasing quantities for building use; as roundwood, it is the preferred wood for pulp, especially groundwood pulp, and for particleboards. On the farm, sawnwood is best used out of ground contact but small poles can be treated to give a reasonable life for fencing.

Western hemlock (*Tsuga heterophylla*)

The wood is very pale brown, non-resinous, not quite as white as spruce and with a more prominent growth ring. It is a little heavier than spruce, is marginally stronger but comparable in stiffness.

Western hemlock dries quickly and well and, when dry, is stable in use. It saws easily and, with sharp tools, takes a good finish; it nails easily but tends to split if the wood is dry. It has a poor resistance to fungi in conditions favouring decay and, like spruce, is difficult to treat effectively with preservatives.

A timber in limited supply from British forests, suitable for the same purposes as spruce. A good building wood in protected environments and sawn for pallets, packaging, etc. For farm and estate purposes, best used out of ground contact, unless given a preservative treatment. Roundwood should be treated if used for poles,

stakes, etc.; it is suitable for pulp and board products.

Western red cedar (*Thuja plicata*)

This has a particularly lightweight wood, non-resinous but with a characteristic smell. Heartwood is pale brown and, except in very young stems, forms a high proportion of the log as there is only a narrow band of pale sapwood. Knots, though frequent, are mostly of small to medium size.

Western red cedar dries quickly and well and when dry is very stable in use. It saws easily but, because it is soft, needs sharp tools to give a good finish. Wet wood corrodes iron, causing a staining of the wood, and, in moist conditions, galvanised or non-ferrous fastenings should be used. It is one of the best British softwoods for resistance to decay, with heartwood lasting 10–15 years in ground contact; sapwood must be treated.

A useful wood, combining good durability and stability, but because supplies of British timber are limited there is no established market. Too weak for house building but suitable for shed and greenhouse framing, staging, seed boxes, and outside facings and claddings. Small roundwood is useful for poles and stakes but should have a preservative treatment.

Printed in the United Kingdom for HMSO
Dd 291296 C35 8/90